MY NAME IS:

_____

I AM

YEARS OLD

A PICTURE OF ME:

WHAT IS THE BEST PART OF BEING EIGHT YEARS OLD?

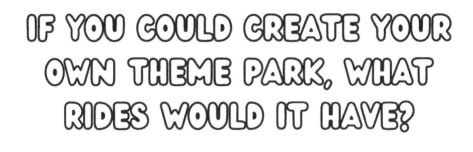

IF YOU COULD CREATE YOUR OWN THEME PARK, WHAT RIDES WOULD IT HAVE?

IF YOU COULD TIME TRAVEL, WOULD YOU VISIT THE PAST OR THE FUTURE?

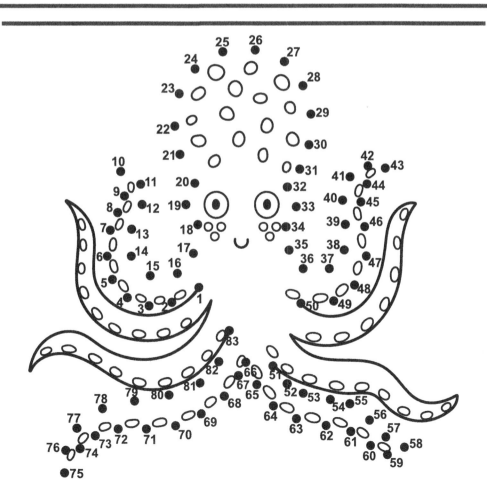

WHAT IS YOUR FAVORITE WAY TO BE CREATIVE?

WHAT IS THE BEST BIRTHDAY YOU EVER HAD?

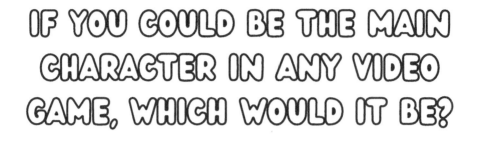

IF YOU COULD BE THE MAIN CHARACTER IN ANY VIDEO GAME, WHICH WOULD IT BE?

WHAT SONG ALWAYS MAKES YOU WANT TO DANCE?

WHAT IS A TALENT OR SKILL YOU WISH YOU HAD?

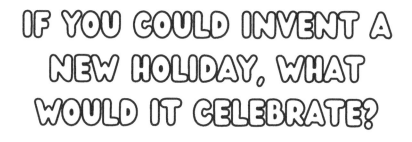

IF YOU COULD INVENT A NEW HOLIDAY, WHAT WOULD IT CELEBRATE?

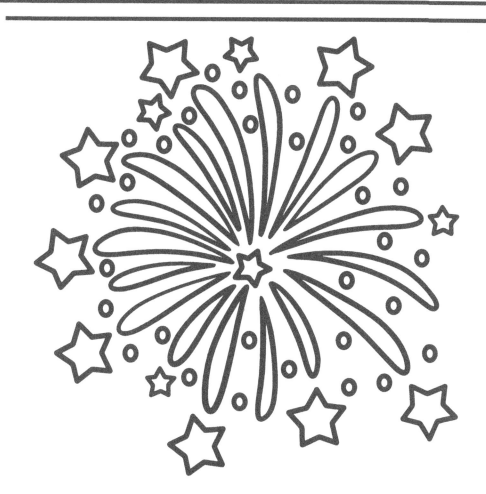

WHAT IS YOUR FAVORITE WAY TO RELAX AFTER A LONG DAY?

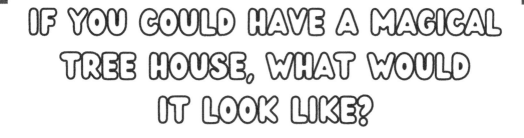

IF YOU COULD HAVE A MAGICAL TREE HOUSE, WHAT WOULD IT LOOK LIKE?

WHAT IS YOUR FAVORITE THING TO DO WITH YOUR FAMILY?

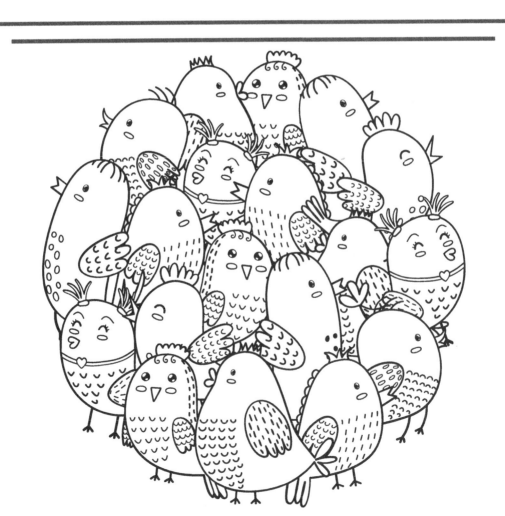

WHAT DO YOU WANT TO BE WHEN YOU GROW UP?

IF YOU COULD GROW ANY PLANT IN YOUR BACKYARD, WHAT WOULD IT BE?

WHAT IS SOMETHING YOU WOULD LIKE TO LEARN HOW TO DO?

IF YOU COULD BE ANY ANIMAL FOR A DAY, WHICH ONE WOULD YOU CHOOSE AND WHY?

IF YOU COULD LIVE ANYWHERE, EVEN IN A FANTASY WORLD, WHERE WOULD IT BE?

WHAT IS A PLACE YOU DREAM OF VISITING ONE DAY?

WHAT IS YOUR FAVORITE BOARD GAME OR CARD GAME?

WHAT IS YOUR FAVORITE MEMORY FROM THE LAST YEAR?

IF YOU COULD WRITE A BOOK, WHAT WOULD THE STORY BE ABOUT?

WHAT MAKES YOU FEEL BRAVE?

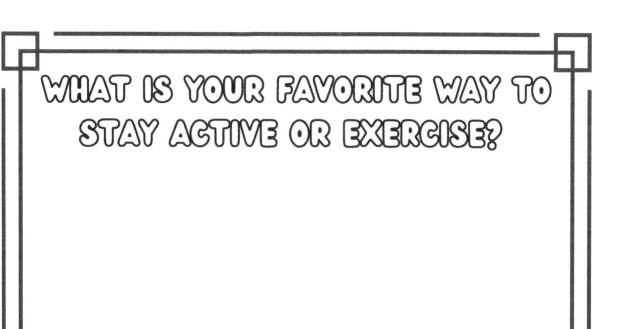

WHAT IS YOUR FAVORITE WAY TO STAY ACTIVE OR EXERCISE?

IF YOU COULD BE FAMOUS FOR ONE THING, WHAT WOULD IT BE?

WHAT IS YOUR FAVORITE THING TO DO IN THE SUMMER?

IF YOU COULD MAKE ANY FOOD HEALTHY, WHAT WOULD IT BE?

IF YOU COULD MAKE ONE WISH COME TRUE, WHAT WOULD IT BE?

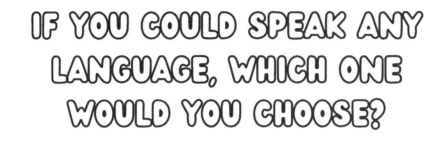

IF YOU COULD SPEAK ANY LANGUAGE, WHICH ONE WOULD YOU CHOOSE?

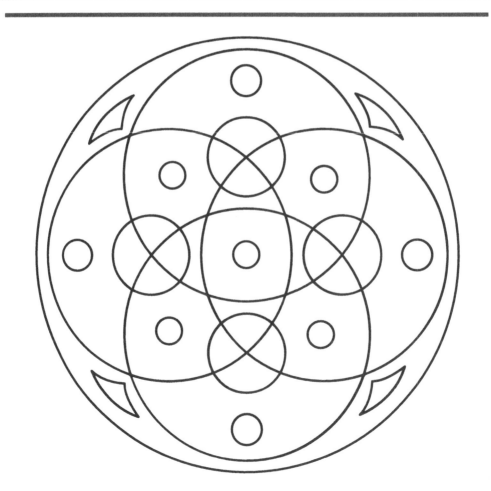

WHAT IS SOMETHING YOU ARE CURIOUS ABOUT AND WANT TO LEARN MORE ABOUT?

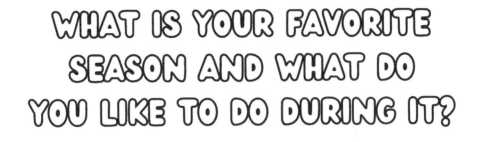

WHAT IS YOUR FAVORITE SEASON AND WHAT DO YOU LIKE TO DO DURING IT?

WHAT IS YOUR FAVORITE TYPE OF WEATHER AND WHY?

WHAT IS THE FUNNIEST MOVIE YOU HAVE EVER SEEN?

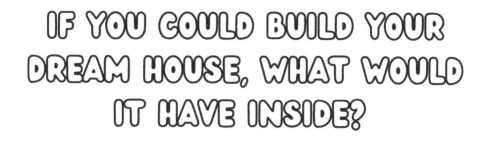

IF YOU COULD BUILD YOUR DREAM HOUSE, WHAT WOULD IT HAVE INSIDE?

WHAT DO YOU LOVE ABOUT YOUR BEST FRIEND?

WHAT IS YOUR FAVORITE MEMORY WITH YOUR GRANDPARENTS OR OLDER RELATIVE?

WHAT IS SOMETHING THAT MAKES YOU LAUGH EVERY TIME?

IF YOU COULD MAKE YOUR OWN TV SHOW, WHAT WOULD IT BE ABOUT?

WHAT IS YOUR FAVORITE THING TO DO WHEN IT IS SNOWING?

WHAT IS THE COOLEST THING YOU HAVE LEARNED IN SCHOOL THIS YEAR?

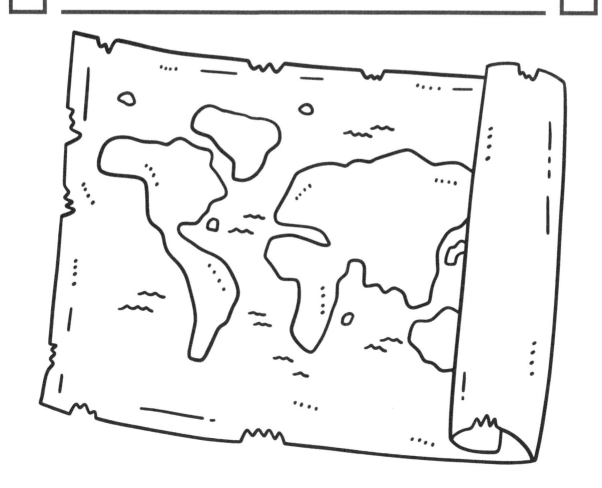

IF YOU COULD HAVE ANY PET, REAL OR IMAGINARY, WHAT WOULD IT BE?

WHAT IS YOUR FAVORITE SUBJECT IN SCHOOL AND WHY?

IF YOU COULD INVENT A NEW BOARD GAME, HOW WOULD YOU PLAY IT?

IF YOU COULD CREATE A NEW SCHOOL SUBJECT, WHAT WOULD IT BE?

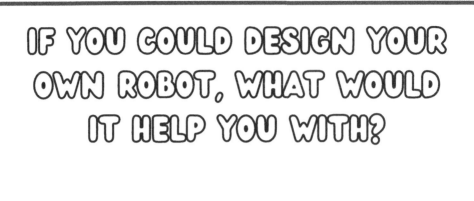

IF YOU COULD DESIGN YOUR OWN ROBOT, WHAT WOULD IT HELP YOU WITH?

WHAT IS YOUR FAVORITE BOOK AND WHAT DO YOU LOVE ABOUT IT?

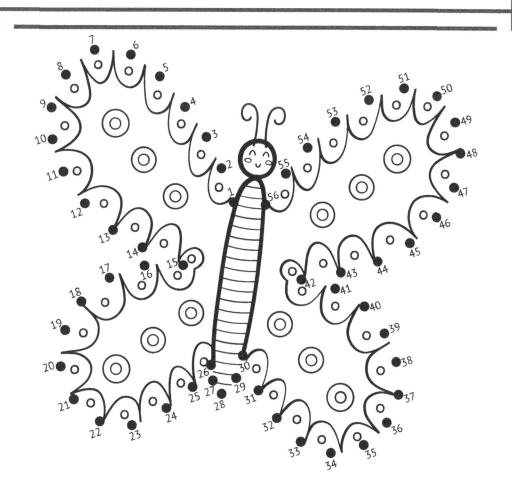

WHAT IS YOUR FAVORITE WAY TO HELP SOMEONE FEEL BETTER?

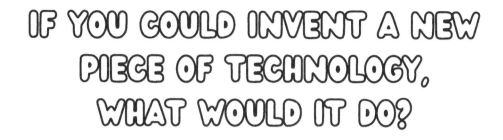

IF YOU COULD INVENT A NEW PIECE OF TECHNOLOGY, WHAT WOULD IT DO?

IF YOU COULD LIVE IN ANY MOVIE, WHICH ONE WOULD YOU CHOOSE?

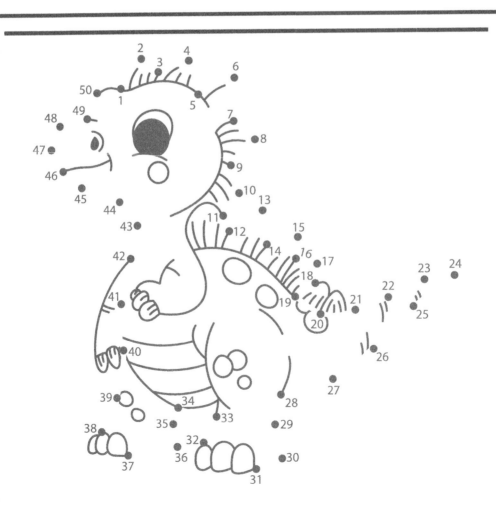

WHAT IS YOUR FAVORITE MEAL AND WHY?

WHAT IS YOUR FAVORITE SPORT OR GAME TO PLAY?

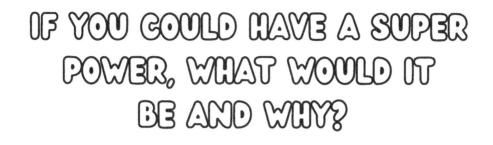

IF YOU COULD HAVE A SUPER POWER, WHAT WOULD IT BE AND WHY?

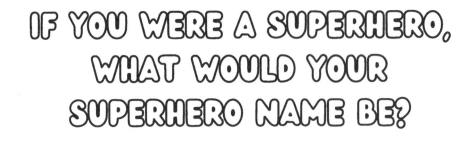

IF YOU WERE A SUPERHERO, WHAT WOULD YOUR SUPERHERO NAME BE?

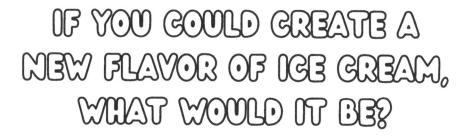

IF YOU COULD CREATE A NEW FLAVOR OF ICE CREAM, WHAT WOULD IT BE?

IF YOU COULD INVENT A NEW TYPE OF TRANSPORTATION, WHAT WOULD IT LOOK LIKE?

WHAT IS YOUR FAVORITE THING ABOUT YOUR FAMILY?

IF YOU COULD HAVE DINNER WITH ANY FICTIONAL CHARACTER, WHO WOULD IT BE?

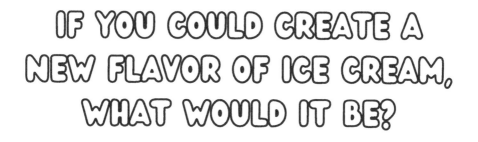

IF YOU COULD CREATE A NEW FLAVOR OF ICE CREAM, WHAT WOULD IT BE?

IF YOU COULD MAKE YOUR OWN TV SHOW, WHAT WOULD IT BE ABOUT?

IF YOU COULD DESIGN A NEW ANIMAL BY MIXING TWO ANIMALS TOGETHER, WHAT WOULD IT BE?

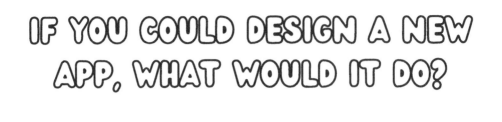

IF YOU COULD DESIGN A NEW APP, WHAT WOULD IT DO?

IF YOU COULD EXPLORE OUTER SPACE, WHICH PLANET WOULD YOU VISIT FIRST?

IF YOU COULD CREATE A NEW CARTOON, WHAT WOULD IT BE ABOUT?

WHAT IS YOUR FAVORITE WAY TO SPEND THE WEEKEND?

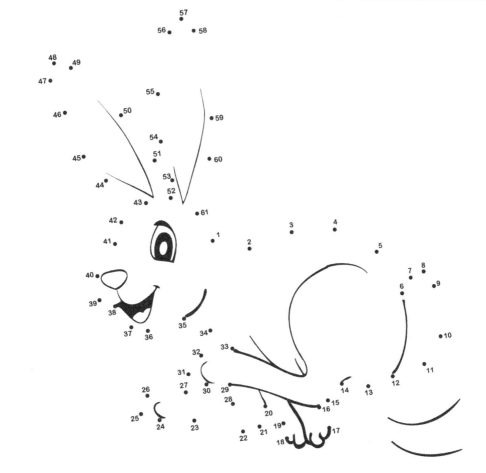

IF YOU COULD MEET ANY FAMOUS PERSON, WHO WOULD IT BE?

WHAT IS YOUR FAVORITE THING TO DO WHEN IT IS SUNNY OUTSIDE?

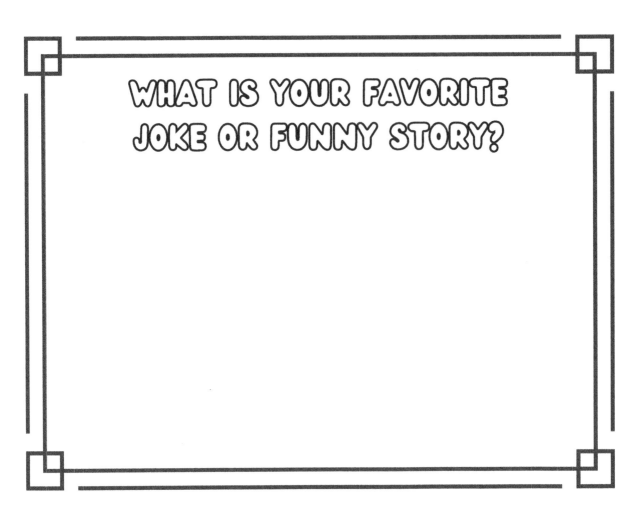

WHAT IS YOUR FAVORITE JOKE OR FUNNY STORY?

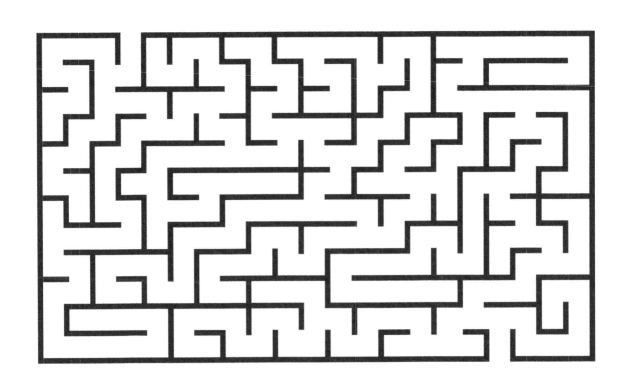

WHAT IS THE MOST FUN YOU HAVE EVER HAD AT THE PLAYGROUND?

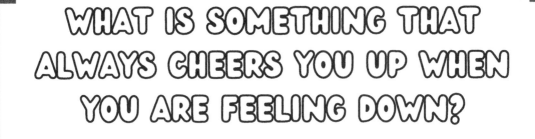

WHAT IS SOMETHING THAT ALWAYS CHEERS YOU UP WHEN YOU ARE FEELING DOWN?

WHAT IS YOUR FAVORITE THING TO DO WITH YOUR FRIENDS?

IF YOU HAD A PET DRAGON, WHAT WOULD YOU NAME IT?

IF YOU COULD SWITCH PLACES WITH ANY CHARACTER FROM A BOOK, WHO WOULD IT BE?

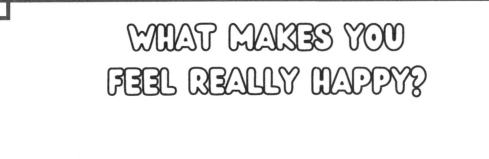

WHAT MAKES YOU FEEL REALLY HAPPY?

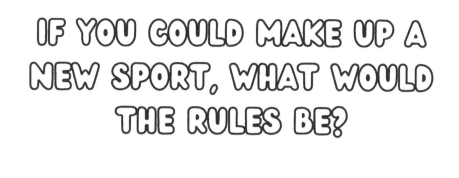

IF YOU COULD MAKE UP A NEW SPORT, WHAT WOULD THE RULES BE?

WHAT IS THE SILLIEST THING YOU HAVE EVER DONE?

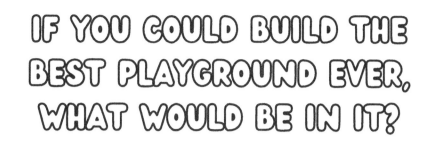

IF YOU COULD BUILD THE BEST PLAYGROUND EVER, WHAT WOULD BE IN IT?

Made in the USA
Las Vegas, NV
04 February 2025

17486685R00044